BURNING THE MAID:

POEMS FOR JOAN OF ARC

BY MARCY HEIDISH

A Woman Called Moses
a novel based on the life of Harriet Tubman

The Secret Annie Oakley
a novel about the legendary sharpshooter

Witnesses
a novel based on the life of Anne Hutchinson

Miracles
a novel on Mother Seton, 1st American Saint

Deadline
a novel of suspense

The Torching — The Bookstore Murders
a novel of supernatural suspense

A Dangerous Woman: Mother Jones, Unsung American Heroine
a novel of a self-proclaimed Hell Raiser

Destined To Dance
a novel about Martha Graham

Scene Through A Window
a historical romance novel

ALSO BY MARCY HEIDISH

Who Cares? Simple Ways YOU Can Reach Out
caring in our immediate circles of concern...

A Candle At Midnight
for those caught in a mental midnight

Soul And The City
finding peace within the rush of the city

Defiant Daughters: Christian Women of Conscience
trail-blazers confronting crises of conscience

Too Late To Be A Fortune Cookie Writer
poems addressing universal concerns of
maturity, mortality, memory and more.

BURNING THE MAID:

POEMS FOR JOAN OF ARC

BY

MARCY HEIDISH

Dolan & Associates, Publisher

BURNING THE MAID: POEMS FOR JOAN OF ARC

Copyright © 2014 by Marcy Heidish

LIBRARY OF CONGRESS CATALOGING-IN-PUBLICATION DATA

Heidish, Marcy.

Library of Congress Control Number: 2014943344

ISBN: 978-0-9905262-0-9

Cover: *Joan of Arc*: oil on parchment; date between
1450 and 1500; current location: Paris, France
Archives Nationales; interpreted by the Wikimedia
Foundation as a faithful photographic reproduction of
a two-dimensional, public domain work of art.

Dolan & Associates, Publisher
Printed in the United States of America
....
First edition

To The Unknown Joans

When I was thirteen
I had a Voice from God.
It was noon
in my father's garden.
The voice came to my right
near the church.
There was a great Light.
      —Jehanne d'Arc

Miracle is the dear child of faith.
      —Frederich Schiller

CONTENTS

AUTHOR'S NOTE

Why another look at Joan of Arc, the subject of historians, biographers, dramatists, and novelists for centuries?

My reasons, in part, are personal. Joan was my earliest heroine and her story led me to write the stories of other women whose courage was costly. I wished to join the ongoing conversation about a magnetic figure and enduring role model.

This collection is *not* an historical novel nor a linear story. Here I hoped to approach Joan of Arc from a different angle: poetry. These offerings are imaginative reflections on aspects of an icon's life: one which still moves and inspires us today.

HISTORICAL CONTEXT

Joan (Jehanne) d'Arc was born about 1412 in the small rural village of Domremy in northeast France. Some sources give her precise date of birth as January 6th. Her farming family was hard-working, illiterate, and devout in its Catholicism.

As the Hundred Years War dragged on, England occupied much of France and French Burgundians collaborated with the invaders. The country was divided, oppressed, and desperate. A complex dynastic dispute weakened its leadership and its armed forces were in disarray. No king had been crowned at Reims, the traditional coronation site, and Orléans, key to the Loire Valley, was buckling under a long siege.

Orléans was critically important to the French for another reason. While it was in enemy hands, Orléans blocked the way to Reims, the traditional site of valid coronations. Joan knew she had to clear the way to Reims Cathedral.

Against this backdrop, Joan's peasant family lived in relatively stability (in a stone house), although Domremy had suffered periodically at the hands of English soldiers. With her brothers, Joan helped with the farming chores and assisted in tending the livestock. From her mother, Joan learned to sew and to say traditional prayers. She ended an engagement but showed no signs of instability or unusual behavior.

At thirteen, in her father's garden, Joan believed she heard "a word from God " and saw "a great light." Later came visions of divine beings. Meanwhile, Joan's voices, or her "counsel," called her to save France from English occupation and oppression. She must lift the siege of strategic Orléans and clear the way to Reims where the heir apparent could be legitimately crowned. The presence of a reigning king would unify a fractured land into a nation.

Joan of Arc showed no signs of mental instability or illness as she grew up, as she led troops, or as she endured months of inquisition during which she gave quick-witted and logical answers. Mysticism has manifested itself in the lives of other illustrious persons from Blake and Carl Jung, Pascal to Harriet Tubman, Dag Hammarskjold and Florence Nightingale.

Joan convinced local officials and soldiers to allow her passage to the court at Chinon. For her own protection, Joan cut her hair and wore men's clothes for this journey and her further military activities. At Chinon, she impressed Charles, the heir to the throne, as yet uncrowned.

Charles believed his demoralized forces would rally behind "The Maid of Lorraine," a legendary figure long predicted to save France in its time of need. Joan never claimed to be this figure but she was often perceived as such. This perception heartened the French military and civilians. In fact, "The Polled Woods, " a forest near Domremy, Joan's home, was where "The Maid" was predicted to appear.

After a clerical examination at Poitiers, Joan was armored as a soldier and given her own banner to rally the troops. In only nine days, Joan led French forces to lift the siege of Orléans. During this struggle she was wounded by an arrow, but after a brief pause she rejoined her forces who took Orléans.

Following this significant victory in May, 1429, Joan continued to lead the French in several other victorious battles in the strategic Loire Valley. Her forces routed the English at Patay. These triumphs cleared the way for the coronation of Charles Vll at Reims Cathedral on July 17, 1429. Several sources report that Joan was an astute military tactician. However, her "counsel" warned her she would only "last a year" before being captured.

With Joan at the forefront again, the French forces began a military campaign to regain Paris from the English. After only one day of fighting, however, the king called a halt to this campaign and revealed a secret truce made with the Burgundian faction, loyal to the English. In the autumn of 1429 Joan was with French forces who took another strategic position.

On December 29, 1429, the king granted Joan and her family nobility status. He then appeared to lose interest in Joan who no longer reported to him. Determined to fight on, she raised her own army. Joan believed she could shorten the 100 Years War which war ended twenty years after her death.

In action at Compiègne, Joan was ambushed and captured by English collaborators, the Burgundians. A large ransom was expected but King Charles made no offers. Joan failed in two attempts to escape her captivity and the Burgundians sold "The Maid" to their allied English forces.

Joan endured a year's imprisonment in a military facility and was interrogated repeatedly by an English sympathizer, Bishop Pierre Cauchon of Beauvais. An ecclesiastical board of inquiry was assembled to determine if Joan's "counsel" came from God or the Devil. Theologians from the University of Paris joined in what was later determined to be a rigged trial for heresy.

In 1431 Joan signed (with an "X") a document she could not read. In it, she "abjured" or denied God sent her on her mission through voices and visions. She had asked for legal counsel but this was consistently denied her. The persistent Bishop Couchon warned her of death by fire if she lapsed. Part of this agreement forbade her to continue to wear male attire. When Joan dressed as a woman she was attacked by guards who attempted rape.

For her own safety, Joan assumed male attire once again. Bishop Cauchon interpreted this action as a relapse into heresy. She abandoned her earlier "abjuration." Although her trial had been irregular on several points, she was condemned to be burned alive.

On May 30, 1431, Joan of Arc was burned at the stake in the market place of Rouen before a large crowd of onlookers. Once she was dead, her blackened body was displayed to prevent any rumors that Joan had escaped. Her body was then burned down to ashes which were then thrown into the Seine so no relics could be made. At the time of her death, Joan was nineteen years old.

Twenty-five years later, in 1456, the doctored transcripts of Joan's trial were examined by a new ecclesiastical tribunal. The case was reopened and no grounds were found for Joan's condemnation and death. The previous trial was also criticized for many "irregularities." The Church in 1456 declared Joan a "martyr" instead of a "heretic." However, she was not beatified until 1909, and not canonized until May 16, 1920, almost five hundred years after her death.

Joan of Arc's leadership and presence enabled France to unite under one king. If Joan had not lifted the siege of strategic Orléans, the English would have gained control of the Loire Valley—and France itself. Many historians see Joan as her nation's savior.

For centuries after her execution "Jehanne" of Domremy has been an inspirational figure to the French people, invoked in wartime and admired in peacetime. This heroine has held scholars and writers in thrall for centuries. She is one of the patron saints of France.

Marcy Heidish

May 30, 2014

PROLOGUE

THIN PLACES

Now the dark drains away
like ink poured into earth

the sky has the color of
a newborn's wide eyes.

It is night day dawn dusk
at this brief timeless time

when a veil thins between
us and what lies beyond.

Thin places thin moments
are sensed seldom seen

they await you in silence
or appear unannounced.

Do not mistake them for
daydreams or fantasies

but you will demand to
know what is their use?

The same use as wheels
ever moving us forward

and roads speeding us
beyond rising horizons.

BEGINNING

HEARING VOICES

Why did I know it wasn't the wind
or a traveler's song on the road
or a farmer's call from his field?

It was a voice more than a voice
and it went through me as one
long note of music pierces air

Listening I tasted honey at first
then the arid ashes of fear my
knees melting underneath me

In my father's garden I saw that
fierce white light like a grounded
star I wanted to run and to stay

From my knotted apron tumbled
the plums I had gathered that
warm yellow summer morning

And me standing silent and still
as a rock in the wall until the
voice and the light faded out

Then I knew what I know now—
they were not the wind or sun
nor my dreams or imaginings

I never doubted it happened
but I vowed to keep the thing
secret maybe a day or a year

Too precious was this to cramp
into words or even confession
wherever it would be scorned

Sensible sober steady am I
not mad not given to spells
not fanciful firm in my faith

And I heard what I heard
And I saw what I saw

JOAN'S ANGELS EXPLAIN

We are the spaces
surrounding the stars
the instant between
flicker and flame

before there was Time
glaciers sand garbage
when earth was
younger still

God spoke us into life
from Him it flows out
like plasma like sap
like mothers' milk

streaming through us
come His messages
though rarely are
they opened

the Holy One made
us holy we watch
over indigo seas and
voyaging souls

we have watched you
a bulb in the womb
born with the grace
of a tulip

a sturdy child you
sat in the garden
butterflies landing
on your slim wrist

your crow-black hair
fell to your waist and
curtained in that hair
you gave thanks

and bent to the ground
as the grasses brushed
your heated face
with green wands

you watched birds skim
the invisible air
trusting the unseen
Holy One

God seemed closer
than your fingertips
you gave to Him
your heartbeats

but surrender is
only for lovers
who must give all
is that you?

SAINTS WATCHING JOAN

she listened
from the first it was so
she heard the creaking
bones of an old orchard
where she would wander
alone always alone and

she heard
the wind as it sang
to her through the leaves
and the trees' pulses
the furling feathers
of flight-worn birds

she watched
as she went about tasks
in her father's house
sewing daily by the fire
the red scribble of noise
she wanted to scrub out

she noticed
the earth rising to her
when she knelt for the
Angelus bell at midday
and saw a stillness
hanging in bright air

she knew
we were there without
knowing she knew it
before we ever spoke
before she replied
and the future unspooled

she sensed
it rolling faster still no
stopping it then and
she saw the end
from the beginning
still she said *Yes.*

JOAN'S CHILDHOOD RHYMES

Days bled together a blur
of eggs to fry pots to stir
deep immensity of night
thimble's flash in firelight
seeds to plant hogs to kill

Does a bud know if it will
become a pea or peony?
Did I know who I'd be?

I felt God hovering near
still to come as yet unclear
something waited to unfold
and undo all that I was told.
I could never be a wife.

She's too quiet for a child
some said but I was wild
inside and bold and strong
for a girlchild this was wrong
but I was gazing far beyond

village fields fences ponds
to what was on its way to me
come quickly to set me free

The watching stars were wise
like a thousand thousand eyes
their paths taught me, Joan,
to move through the Unknown
Did they see the Secret in me?

Papa looked me over carefully.
This odd child, I heard him say,
but I smiled and looked away.

ON FAITH

Maybe it falls over you
like sun through a veil
like a dusting of pollen

the tree's green heft
reaching through me
rising past my knees

Or does it flatten you
like lightning's arrows
a storm's slam of hail?

branching now taller
flexing and leafing
roots stronger still

For some so it comes
such things I've heard
no bush burned for me

each yearning year
a trunk grew in rings
as I became that tree

Faith seeded my soul
fed by pain joy prayer
growing like an oak

and it became me
body and branches
without my asking

it is who I am and I
am what it is and it
will live on after me

FIRE

Drawn to you young
as a child in a church
I am watching you now
still straining to touch
the untouchable hem
of your flaring skirts

you move in an endless
dance with the dark
down the hallways
of time you leap
despite the night's weight

you take to yourself
stories spells songs
chanted ages ago
bearing them all into
the future even as
you gather us now

to look at your face
and tell sacred tales
and rest at your side
you who lived before
you will outlive us

I don't fear you yet.

MIRACLES

The dark descends
with a long black sigh
to cool the feverish air
moistening dry ground
with its maligned mercy

in night's darkest core
in its secret marrow
hidden from daylight's
long probing fingers
its unblinking eyes

miracles open like night-
blooming flowers often
unseen understood
but they scent the air
before we notice

they blossom while
we pass their borders
and smell their perfume
tonight we can't guess
when a miracle opens

like the night-blooming
flowers scenting damp
air under our windows
as we close the shutters
and put out the lights

THE VOICES RETURN

Waiting
she stands mute
her red dress
a wineskin
enclosing not
pouring her
blood.

Waiting
she stands still
within a green
chapel of trees
branches leaning
bent in praise of
God.

Waiting
she listens
to her mother
slicing onions
father tramping in
for supper to say
Grace.

Waiting
to be told when
it was time for her
to arrow through
the darkness
fleeing home
alone.

Waiting
each new morning
she hopes it will
be today she dives
into tomorrow
repeating her
Yes.

Waiting
she looked up
at our brightness
like a lantern
hanging from
the silent
air.

Waiting
patience slips now
soon the secret's
seal will open
let it be soon
let the end begin.

LISTEN

Words curl in the air
all falling like leaves
unfurling green lives

they whisper secrets
laughing like children
then deeper rustlings

attend to their stories
as ripening peaches
cling to a branch

watch words scatter
like October leaves to
spill in your pathways

winter's bare branches
are not stripped of words
these speak through birds

words tumble around you
as skies lean and listen to
tales they forgot to recall

the stars hear each word
ever invented and so they
will when we are long mute

this is how grace arrives
in a shower of word-leaves
God spoke them into being

IF

If you can float on a lake
fingered by air
if you can lean on the sea's
heaving greenness
if you can drift off on music
never visible

If you can float on night's
black buoyancy
you can ride on its edge
and sink deep into
its untouchable darkness
without holding on

If you can do this you can
rest in God's palm
unseen but firm as a new
mattress waiting to
bear your heavy dreams
even as you sleep

JOAN ANSWERS HER VOICES

Yes yes I hear you
always when you speak

I hear you see you now
as I wait listen watch

At last it is time you say
and you will guide me

Your words cover me
like sunlight on snow

I understand plainly
what where why now

Free Orlèans you say
then crown the king

It is clear it is soon
it is mine to accept

I will miss this garden
our pear tree's shade

Even so I go smiling
for this was I born

All will be shown me
your promise I trust

I hoped for this hour
and now it is come

Papa thinks I'm daft
I don't mind let it be

Whenever you leave
me I am sorrowful

But you will return
I can't do it alone

I await what is next
must you go now?

JOAN'S FATHER SPEAKS

My daughter is crazy
she talks to the pear tree
some say she's holy
some say she's witched

of one thing I'm certain
she needs a whipping
and that she will have
when I finish supper

we are simple folk
nor can we read so
this foolishness is
not from some book

but you can't stop the
tellers of tales they're
a dangerous lot able
to turn a girl's head

look at her, will you,
her body is here but
her mind such as it is
has strayed far away

she looks sane enough
even so and she is
pious and we know the
possessed cannot pray

just past fourteen she is
and may fancy some lad
I'd rather have her crazy
than have her pregnant

so people think she's
the Maid of Lorraine
the savior of France
and its downtrodden

and this prediction has
slid down the ages from
Merlin himself but he
didn't name her Joan

I damn well did that on
her baptismal day and
I didn't spawn no legend
to live under my roof.

SUFFERING FRANCE

The sky is weeping on
the shoulders of houses
and the houses' thin skins

before there were houses
the sky was weeping
on the trees' green eyelids

before there were forests
the sky was weeping
on the skulls of stone caves

before there were caves
the sky was weeping
on the pain of all people

before there was pain
before there was France
the sky alone knows

before there was sky
there was God only God
and his breath of mercy

THE MAID OF LORRAINE

On Sunday evenings
the week empties its
waste into this hole
dug in the ground

Here we poor people
trudge after dark falls
to dig through a pile
of reeking garbage

old bread old cheese
fish-heads lost grapes
maybe a shoe or two
it has been this way

since the enemy came
taking over our villages
setting houses aflame
stealing horses and cows

we are a proud people
not broken until now
the enemy made us
stinking scavengers

as we dig we still pray
O God let her come
as it was predicted—
The Maid of Lorraine

in that forest she waits
for the hour to appear
making us who we were
delivered from digging

God frees his people
it has always been so
He parted the seas he
led slaves to new land

May He send to us now
the promised savior of
France we eat scraps
and pray till she comes

is she now among us?
Does she see us here?
Do we see her there?
Can it be Jehanne?

CONFESSION

Joan: In the Name of the Father—

Priest: Yes, yes, go on, child.

Joan: Bless me Father for I have—

Priest: Yes, yes, your sins?

Joan: Uncharitable thoughts...

Priest: About your brothers again?

Joan: Yes, Father, they're so loud.

Priest: That is not a sin.

Joan: Three times I almost cursed.

Priest: What did you almost say?

Joan: Sacre Blue!

Priest: That is not a curse. And—?

Joan: I looked at a boy in church.

Priest: You had impure thoughts?

Joan: I wondered why he looked at me.

Priest: Child, how old are you now?

Joan: Thirteen, Father, I think.

Priest: You come three times a week.

Joan: Yes, Father. Is that wrong?

Priest: Too often for you, for anyone.

Joan: I feel I need Confession.

Priest: You wish to be pure?

Joan: Worthy, Father, only that.

Priest: To be a good wife, no doubt.

Joan: My penance, Father?

Priest: Pick flowers and sing.

ENGAGEMENT

I broke it off—
our sealed betrothal—
so you know that now.
My father's shamed
rage is a lash to me
but it is your sorrow
that pains me when
you say I cause your
bright spirit to weep.

I cannot now do as
the other girls will
I cannot love you
God and France
all together all three.
I can only hold onto
one love at a time
and my time is short.

You think me an oak
in glorious leaf
but I am the spinach
in my father's garden
I am the moss on the
stones by the stream
I am footprints in soil.

False modesty? Not
so, dear one, not so.
I know what I am and
I am not your dream.
Don't seek me at fairs
or frolic or at a feast
Don't seek me at home
with my distaff in hand.

Soon I leave Domremy
but I also remain
Find me in the fields
in the plowed earth in
pitched hay and roses
Look for me here even
when you think me gone

I will wear your wound
like a stain on the shift
under my dress my cloak
this stain won't wash out
whatever you suppose
whatever you will hear
Remember I am but a
spring bloom never to
ripen into summer fruit.

RISING

LAST GLANCE

I want to remember

the pasture's blue haze
where our cows float
as if at sea

above
the clouds white-gold
throwing shadows
across watery grass

meadows
of wild flowers
gold as a cat's eyes
lighting the meadows

fields
set off by long rock walls
ancient stones like skulls
laid by hands gone to dust

light
in a barrel of rain
silvering blades of tall grass
around papa's plow

beneath
in this earth lie
long-buried bones
ribs shins arms

below
knives and blades
a rake a man's jaw
blood fed this land

pushing
past blades and bones
a spring rises now
it spurts breaking ground

the barn
yields a new calf's cry
priests bless the crops
they grow reaching high

Let me look again
one final glance
I gather it to me
I want to remember

I want to remember

LEAVING HOME

Tonight it begins
Running off to the town
Never to see this house
again

Now I see amber light
pock the long scarred table
Wooden bowl spilling
plums

Boiling pot Smell of stew
Banging wooden shutters
opening the day Morning's
milk

Bunched dandelions
in a mug on the mantel
Crackle of lit kindling's
fire

People speak sing cough
brothers mother Papa
village footsteps voices
calling

I want to go I want to stay
one day only that one
in this old stooping
house

Tomorrow I wake in the dark
to breathe in our land
green sleeping seeds
growing

Night will drain away
like ink poured into earth
the sky's eyes opening
gray-blue

And I must be gone then
running away to my life
to the strong soft hands of
God

I leap now into the sun-fed unknown
make me light humble strong
O God of peace who calls me to war
harvest me hasten me hear me now

COURAGE

Its skin is what
you first note about
courage
never its core
nor its heft nor its form
but the peel the rind
the binding
itself of the juice and
the flesh of the fruit.

It is the skin
sealing the body of
courage
until it is needed and it
gives itself over to you
but it is a fruit
you seek in secret
and never name.

It is your skin
that is risked when
courage
is needed to fight
an enemy
be it death be it life
be it human in form
be it you.

Its skin is what
you first touch when you find
courage
within your mind
within your soul
within you it grows.

SACRIFICE

To her waist once flowed Joan's hair
the color of night with a half-moon
Stealing away she saw its reflection
in pails in water in rare window glass
Confessing in silence her sly vanity.

Where the willows wept into a stream
Joan washed her hair flinging it out
Kneeling when the hair lay before her
to dry in July the best month for sun
Lingering brushing it sleek as a cat.

Now she rides toward her new life
Knowing she must cut off her hair
must take on the form of a soldier
must look like a man among men
must do it now before any regrets.

Waking early she murders her prize
her pride and her pearl of great price
Her weapon a knife honed like a bone
she chops the hair short as if dicing
an onion—but no tears—it is done.

Joan watching her hair like silk ribbons
drift on a stream blessing its strands
thankful for their growing their being
their going away with all childish things
No more foolery now Time to ride on.

PILGRIMAGE

These old dirt roads
may thicken like honey
or fragment like salt
sprinkled by the sun

a simple walk, it seems,
the sky is a blue circus tent
its tough strings tethered
to a distant red lighthouse

each shaggy path is lined
with guardian junipers
ink-dark umbrellas in rain
and at noon but they know

what you soon will learn—
this walk never ends and
never remains simple
just when you're striding

a flat road spikes steeper
and sometimes you crawl
drinking the dust but
comrades rise beside you

to watch for pitfalls
dragons thieves even so
remember to sing as you go
and above all—tell stories

Stories alone pave the road.

CHARLES, ROYAL HEIR, RECEIVES JOAN

Who is she, I wonder, this odd girl,
what gives her an unearthly air:
warrior's eyes in the face of a nun,
and a quietness all about her as
if she were cut from a cloud.

It doesn't make sense, this shine
to a shepherdess, only a peasant,
sturdy but pensive and proud
by looks older than seventeen;
maybe she lies as women will?

And yet she made my best men
bring her to me here at court, not
by seduction nor feminine tricks,
nor by the feminine beauty that
stops the heart, no, not that sort.

They say she is the awaited one,
the Maid of Lorraine, predicted
by wise men to rise from those
forests beyond her own home
to wrest us from enemy hands.

Why don't I test her? We are
so desperate what can I lose?
I could allow her to rally what's
left of my army and lead them.
Can a legend be true? Why not?

THE SENDING

When it happens as hoped
when it goes as you prayed
why does the sky not sing?
why do the trees not dance?

I will sing dance praise God
I will offer thanks to my Lord
It is done and I am approved
it is The Maid who leads now

they lay heavy armor on me
vesting a girl like a bishop
in steel they give me a sword
though I am but a peasant

and this I always remember
and this is what centers me
I am one of my soldiers and
I am one *with* each soldier

we ride out to fight for France
and as we ride we *are* France
from fields towns farms cities
from this soil we come as one

war is not glory war is of Hell
war is no brave tale no song
I have seen the bloodied dead
I have seen the price to be paid

Let there be a blanket of peace
Let there be a mantle of quiet
Falling over torn land torn limbs
Falling from God's healing hand

I will not live to see this, I know
I will not last more than one year
But one year can change twenty
Let me embrace this day.

And so I begin.

ONWARD TO ORLÉANS

Am I who I was or who I am—
a warrior wielding a sword?

A slip of a girl, a snip of a girl,
sewing last spring by the fire

cut from the cloth of a woman
clothed in the chainmail of man

I wait within this suit of armor
like a chalice I glint in the sun

but inside my heavy steel skin
breathes a soft curving figure

unwilling to tremble or weaken
forbidden to weep or show fear

behind me 5,000 men gather
all eyes on the banner I raise

and I abandon that other Joan
she is left alone in the fields

the warrior maid takes her place
ready now to lead her brothers

she sets her face for Orléans
raised at her like a stone fist

with these men she will take it
with the Holy One she can

sword lifted she orders the charge:
For God for France for the Maid!

UNTAMED

Do not think me sweet
as the peaches I plucked

Mistake me not for a
soft feather bed

Never see me as tame
as a dove in a nest

I am bossy and brash
now more than ever

In retreat and in war
my soldiers know it

with each victory I will
grow stronger and so

I dictate this letter bound
to a fast arrow and this

have launched behind
our enemy lines:

You have no right to be
in France so be warned

the King of Heaven is
with us to send you word

by me Jehanne the Maid—
depart to your own land

or I will raise such a war-cry
as to be remembered forever...

And that is not all I will say
nor is that my last arrow

VICTORIES AT ORLÉANS

My soul doth magnify the Lord
Now it is done—what can I say?

My spirit rejoices in God my Savior
as I accept the Virgin Mary's words?

He has regarded the humility
my girlish peasant self

of His lowly handmaiden
my poor words rise to you

He who is mighty has done
more than I deserve and

great things for me Holy is He
all I can offer as my thanks

He gives the hungry good things
I give you the sum of who I am

the rich He sends empty away
and they will leave France

His mercy endures from
our birth beyond life itself

generation to generation
even if you ask my life

my spirit rejoices
my spirit rejoices

Amen
Amen

THE ARROW

When the arrow hit
it bit me like a snake
it struck like lightning.

My body sang with pain,
a song it never knew before
and I wept like a child not

like the soldier I must be.
The shame of it, the shame,
and my cry to God: *Why*?

As the men wrenched the
arrow out of my shoulder
the answer came to me:

Why should I be protected?
Why not suffer with the others?
What arrogance to think I was
excused from human agony?

I stand I am steady
I raise my banner and
again mount my horse
Ride On, I call, *Ride On*

JOAN'S VOICES ON HER TRIUMPH

We saw this moment hurling
through spiraled seasons
circles within cycles
wheeling centuries

arrowing through layered veils
of dust and ash and dew
falling stars and comets
spinning meteors

launched by God's right hand
it makes a silent landing
on course and on time
shining on the Maid.

Te Deum Laudamus Domine
shouts Joan from her horse
O God we praise Thee Lord
upheld to Him her sword
glinting in her hand

Sun bouncing off her armor
and silvering this girl whose
gleam is like a chalice
bearing grace

Bell's tongues chiming and
the cheering troops and
townspeople of Orléans
singing thanks

While Joan retreats alone
to give herself again to God
knowing it is not she
creating this day

Te Deum Laudamus Domine
whispering it now she thinks
how quiet she feels within
how still how hushed
it must be this way.

A SEASON OF GRACE

Sometimes it comes that way
pouring like wine from a bottle

grace falls over us as we ride
town after town opens to us

fists become upturned palms
peaceful surrenders our gifts

this year roses bloom longer
grass greener skies nearer

at dawn the sun is a peach
as day wanes light lingers

town after town bows to us
massy trees open their arms

the enemy says I'm a witch
that explains these victories

they do not see God's hand
can work through a woman

but I care not I have much
to do and my time is short

grace pours like wine now
but bottles always empty

so I drink in every day
as if I lacked for another

and when that happens I
will remember this wine

RETREAT

I am not done with you,
Paris, oh no, not yet.

For now we fall back
but no fall is forever.

I was headstrong as
always a willful girl

at home or in battle
my brothers swear it.

This day I was wrong
to press on to Paris.

Too much did I crave
that city's crest.

Perhaps it was pride
driving me forward,

Not Heaven's King
but worldly winning.

Temptation is tricky
out here on the field

I heard no Voices to
say *march* or *delay*;

Trouble awaits when
I seek my own way

CAPTAIN LAHIRE REMEMBERS

There was a softness to her
few people saw the air of
a woman risen from a bath.
As she spoke of home her
voice was naked and new.

She would draw into herself,
still as a windless morning,
and her face would appear
lit from within, like the moon
in a cloud; Joan at prayer.

No soldier likes admitting
to softness, nor did she, but
it fed her strength as a well
feeds the land if you know
how to dig—and Joan did.

Before a battle, she moved
among her men, sensing
furled fears with uncanny
ease and she, a torch, set
brave rage in each mind.

Exacting, impatient, asking
us all she asked of herself,
maybe too much, but when
she led a charge we'd ride
into hell for her and France.

And she, fighting wounded,
twice that was, felt the force
of her army behind her and
when she raised her banner
we knew we'd fight on.

THE KING'S CORONATION

I am a pealing bell
and no one can hear
me except God

Swinging on thin air
I scatter my sound
and God listens

My tongue is a long
tail of a comet but
only God sees

This chiming of mine
tells today's news
and thanks God

What was promised
is here is now is done
as God had planned

The king is crowned
France is saved God
sings through me

This is not my doing
I am only a bell for
our God to ring

I am not noticed now
by His Royal Majesty
but God still sees me

No longer needed is
Jehanne the Maid
but God knows me

I am yet needed and
I will fight until God
stops me from ringing

KING CHARLES AFTER HIS CORONATION

Oh please
Not her again
I'll pour my wine
into a piss-pot
if I hear that name
one more time.

The Maid of Orlèans
they call her since
that stunning victory
yes I'll give her that
but the glory rightly
goes to me.

True enough
I was not there but
for me the army fought
it was my royal name
leading us to triumph
you must agree.

This lowly peasant girl
cannot write her name
and yet that name has
the sheen of sorcery
drawing all men to her
like an idol.

Worse still
they say that virgin girl
made **ME** the monarch
crowned at Reims and
yes she cut a path for me
now I reign.

I do not need her anymore
the savior (they like to say)
of **My** realm **My** France
how can a lass command
My armies?

Theft of glory Joan will pay
I will let her self-destruct
as certainly she shall
the clergy will see to it her
time is short.

Then watch my splendor
awe them all as I loose
my lightning on the sky
and light up France don't
ask me why.

NIGHT

It is late but the dark is young
the houses on this street
are closing their eyes
the trees shift in slumber
and in their murmured dreams

and I sit within a bowl of night
conformed to its curves
where I wait for words
to spill into the bowl
if I remain silent and listen

for the sibilant sound they create
to signal their presence
they are quiet by nature
first heard in the mind
amplified by our daylight voices

but here in night's bowl the words
slip in like a whisper
outside a lover's window
even the hard words
with muscular heft begin in this way

though I sit in the dark I watch for
the words' different colors
older than time fresh as milk
not yet formed from new grass
brighter than sun in the bowl of night

FALLING

JOAN'S CAPTURE AT COMPIÈGNE

And suddenly it ends
so quick so rough.
My voices warned me
but I wanted more time.

Abrupt, a shock, a blow,
this battlefield attack
as we were in retreat—
only for the day, one day.

I did not see them coming,
men who dragged me off,
tearing me from my mount,
making me their captive.

Worth a king's ransom—
so they cried and crowed
but there was no ransom
nor did I wait, expectant.

Did God allow this trap?
Or was it the Devil's work?
No doubts ever pricked me
not until this grim gray day.

Now I will be sold off
like a horse or a house
and to the dread enemy:
our invaders, the English.

This I fear above all things,
these English and allies
They see me as a witch.
And witches are burned.

I fear little enough on earth
Fire, only, brings me terror.
Does it wait to consume me
as I sit here in a dank prison?

JOAN'S VOICES MUSE

Why me?
She never asked, we never said
but she wondered, we know:
Why not choose another girl,
prettier smarter better than me
a girl who could at least read?

Why Joan?
She was of the land of the people
of those who love God
an open door to His mysteries
stubborn and strong-willed and—
passionate this is the key.

Why me?
Joan wondered still.
Why do you let me suffer for God?
Why? We answer her so:
Did your mother give birth easily?
And did Jesus not suffer for thee?

I see.
Why *not* me?

IN PRISON

I will not stay here
like a plate on a shelf
in a cupboard with rats

I will not stay hidden
like a window
behind dusty shutters

I will not stay trapped
like a thumb in a fist
punching the darkness

I speak not from pride
like a damsel in silks
without her comforts

I speak not from rage
like a brawling drunk
who fights like a boy

I know who I am
a peasant's daughter
who can't write her name

I know Who sent me
unschooled as I be
for His own reasons

I know not God's mind
nor does any creature
who tramples the earth

Prison wastes time
and my time is short
a year at the most

DESPAIR

Watch as she paces her cell
ten steps left ten steps right
heels rapping rough stones
like beggars' fists on a door

She thinks we have left her
but now fear deafens Joan
No more escapes only this
prison these chains this wait

Pacing even in her sleep
she sees herself as a child
losing her way in the fields
waves of swaying pale grain

no one to hear her crying out
gone every face footstep hand
fields widening now into waves
drowning the child wading there

no end to the land stretching
out all around her nothing but
tall waving feathers on stalks
No God in this placeless place

the world has yellowed with age
a purpling sky out of reach all
fading now with the day's light
Find me O Jesus are You here

fighting her way through the
black weedy sea she watches
the stars too many to number
uncaring cold fires and stern

but forming familiar patterns
the dipper the hunter the bear
O-God-Somewhere-Up-There
lead me home by Your stars...

Joan lurches awake in her cell
no sky no stars but she calls
O-God-Somewhere-Up-There
and hears sees nothing at all

STILL IN PRISON

This window:

It tempts me to leap
into the blue-eyed day
and stride out to a ledge
of thin and invisible air

But wait:

Do not mistake me
Never would I try
to take my own life
I vow by the saints

My Plan:

Tumble like a leaf
to a soft dry moat
It lies just below I
would land easily

Courage Joan:

A few seconds only
through the bright air
and I am free though
the drop is long

Go Now:

You guide me down
a shaft of Your breath
nothing to fear I fly
always leaning on You.

The Jump:

Air scalding cheeks
wind screaming past
Hail Mary full of Grace
dazed but whole I land

The Landing:

They think I am dead
running to me their
breath reeking onions
they stand me upright

The Ending:

A new prison around me
no window no sky no sun
I acted without my voices
now look what I've done.

IN DOUBT

Why did I think it *wasn't* the wind?
Why *not* a piper out on the road?
Why *not* a man scything in the fields?

Why did I trust those Voices I heard?
Why would they be speaking to *me*?
Why would they be speaking at all?

Why did I think there are miracles now?
Why did I think of the Devil's tricks?
Why did I not suspect I dreamed it?

Why do my sins bite me like ticks?
Why do my mistakes line up in a row?
Why do my nights grow like gray beards?

Why do I keep asking *Why*?

WHAT COUNTS?

Fireflies cut button-holes
of light into the dark
serge of a summer sky.

Rising from tall grasses
others nick the night and
fly, flit, flicker, die.

How can this be done
so casually? I turn to
find out what you see.

In my many Julys, I've
seen generations and
ancestors of fireflies.

"But why can't they last?"
I demand. "My Lord God
tell me why."

"Listen now." God's voice
is clear. "What matters
is the flying, not the dying."

I kick my two feet
three times and, silently,
ashamed, I start to weep.

"Why should they die?"
The answer a surprise:
"Why should they fly?"

INQUISITION

I taste their questions
but do not swallow them
they are all poisoned

Are your Voices
from God or
from Satan?

They serve me more
I taste the poison
but must spit it out

Are you in a state
of grace now
do you know?

Any child can smell
milk that has spoiled
lard turning rancid

Thank God if I am
if not may he
put me there

And I am no child now
I have aged at this
my last supper

Rumbling voices
they hate when
I speak smart

I cannot feed on hate
maggots curl in
bishops' bread

They don't want
my answers they
want my death

days weeks months
of more questions
always the same

O God, let this
Cup pass from me
but your will be done

TRIAL

months blend into one
questions intense now
these men gather here
priests bishops scholars
It is twenty against one

I must sleep in a cage
unless they move me
in shackles and chains
can one peasant girl
be so great a danger?

Bishop Cauchon wants
me burned as a witch
but I ask for a priest
for Holy Communion
what witch asks that?

now I grow weary of
questions and traps
my words matters not
it is already decided
it will go as they wish

Temptation is served
like sweetmeats to me
if I renounce my voices
my visions my mission
they will let me survive

So it always appears
a poisonous sweet I
taste it this time but
I will not swallow now
God help me not yet

The bishop shows me
the stake where I will
die screaming aflame
fear fingers my spirit
and tells me *Live!*

RECANTING

They give me a paper to sign
I cannot read it they know but
this paper will save my life
The bishop readies his quill
and in his ink I sign with an *X*

with that *X* it is done I will live
and I sign one more long paper
the bishop pressed upon me
he holds my hand to write in
my baptized name: *JEHANNE*

in my cell I can't breathe I
am sick I am cold I am hot
because I signed their lies
I feared burning to death but
worse it is to burn with shame

my Voices now chasten me
I denied God and all I believe
when I put my name to lies
it is better to lose your life,
than it is to lose your soul.

A tree cannot live without sap
and I bled out my sap today
a bird cannot fly without wings
and I shed my feathers today
Mea culpa mea maxima culpa

Listen to me O men of the cloth
tear my name from your papers
and go on to kindle the flames
the smoke of my burnt flesh
I offer up now to my God

BURNING

ANGELIC APOLOGIA

Light the fire.
Have it over.
Waiting adds
torture to torture.

Ten thousand souls
gather in Rouen's
market place to see
The Maid burn and

The scaffold is
readied there on
that hill of wood
and yet we wait.

ten thousand stories
and songs will come
of this for centuries
but ours must be first.

We must watch
her ending as we
did her beginning
but we look beyond

that stake where
she will gutter out
like a human candle
while Joan looks at us.

We can see the arc
of Joan's earthly life
so kindle the logs—
Let the ending begin.

THE EXECUTIONER:
ROUEN, 30 MAY 1431

The fire blossoms
a flowering garden
tall tossing lilies
all growing at once
rising and reaching
orange on orange
no horrid scent
to petals of flame
only the stench of
burnt human flesh.

I kindled this blaze
under strict orders
but I will be damned
for giving a saint
smoke for a shroud.
More orders now:
rake back the fire
display the stake
where Joan's body
sags steaming still
charred inky black

Screaming to God
choking she died
crowds weeping but
bishops smiling
they wanted her death.
More orders now:
light the fire again
burning The Maid
down to ashes
dumped in the Seine.

I was pressed into
service at Rouen
I feared saying *No*
this I must confess
but no absolution
can take it away I
will burn my life out
and when I myself
die—what then?

AN ENGLISH SOLDIER:
ROUEN, 30 MAY 1431

Let the witch burn and burn now
lest she use sorcery to escape

This conniving shape-shifter first
woman then man then demon

What else could this young girl be?
The weaker sex cannot win battles

The stupid French have been fooled
but her time is over today at Rouen

Show no mercy for this enchantress
Hasten to burn her out of this world.

JOAN'S MOTHER SPEAKS

I have lived too long because I live to see this day
to watch my daughter like meat at that stake and
for what cause?

Her trial was not a fair one and what, I ask You, was
her crime in leading her country's forces to free
us from our oppressors?

I know she ran away from home to do this thing but
didn't I hear her stealing out and didn't I keep her
father distracted in bed?

Now how can I bear the sight of her turned into a
living torch and how can I bribe a soldier to pull
her from the fire?

O God, will You smother her in smoke before she
burns and will you show me why You allow such
things to happen?

Lord, you are the God of mercy and justice and this
is neither and I ask You how will I have the strength
for prayer again?

Why is the sky slate and Your silence is
glass reflecting a mother's face twisting like
rope into a tight knot?

You know me and You know my devotion
to You all my life but how can You ask
my piety now as You let my daughter burn?

WITNESSES TO THE BURNING

A Peasant:

Damn! She's a farmer's daughter, that's why she
dies. Think they'd burn a duke or a bishop? By my
beard, they would NOT. Joan's one of us, a
peasant. I'll say it, fact is we're treated like dogs,
or worse. This, my friend, is worse. A girl lit like a
candle? May the English burn in Hell.

Another Peasant:

You'd best watch your mouth. If the King's men
hear that you'll be next. And maybe the girl had it
coming. Might have thought herself better than
us, riding around on that white charger, armored
like a man. That's not seemly at all for a woman,
not even a whore. I know, I know, everyone knows
she's a virgin. They checked her, you know? I say,
So what?

A French Soldier:

A finer commander don't live or breathe. I served
the best—the Maid. A magnet, that girl. Is. Was.
We was all drawn to her in spite of ourselves—she
knew when to attack, when to retreat. If you ask
me, she's envied, is what. Headstrong, to be sure
—had to be. Didn't take nothing from no one—
until now.

Domremy Baker's Wife:

Sorry I came. Terrible, this. Knew Joan all my
life. Since she would walk. A child like any other.
Sold her Hot Cross Buns every year. Had her
mother's manners. No witch, this one. Trumped
up charges. Where's the king? Done with her now.
Sorry I came. Can't watch her burn.

Cauchon, Bishop of Beauvais:

Get on with it. I told you, make haste or the
crowds may protest. Look at the simpletons, half
of them weeping, even if they didn't know the
wretched girl. A fraud, that's what she is, that's
what she was, a sly French peasant, I know the
type. I have always been on the right side, the
side of the English. Now then, make haste, burn
the witch down to ashes. I will bring the news to
the King.

A Seamstress of Rouen:

I stitched that white garment she wears and I'm
not proud of that and I only did it out of fear and I
tell you that work was like stitching a shroud for
a child or bride and in a way she was both and
believe me if she wasn't a woman she'd not be
dying today in my gown, my gown.

A Troubadour:

Why are we here? Our troupe makes people laugh
or lulls them with song. This market place is no
stage, it's a scaffold, and I don't like this act. The
English tricked her, I'm sure of that.

JOAN ON THE SCAFFOLD

I am chained to a stake
as if I could climb the air
like a ladder into thin sky
or skip like a child down
the hill of wood awaiting
its first tongues of flame.

One torch to dry kindling
a fringe of fire below me
then a gray veil of haze
growing and then the smoke
a winding sheet wrapping
me layer by layer by layer

thickening rising faster
smoke hiding the crowds
no one can now see my
pale shift or tall hat marked
with bad words I can't read
one I am sure is *HERETIC*.

Soon enough I do not care
I cough and gasp
eyes running lips cracked
bitterness on my tongue
taste of wormwood or gall.

I try to swallow air
and I try to pray but
there is a roar in my ears
can't hear my Voices now
I cry out My God my God
why have You forsaken me?

The blaze climbs nearer
to bite at my feet
I call out Jesus O Jesus
but I am dazed my blood
boils in my veins my head
seems to be floating away.

Drifting off I stare down at
myself but I see only our
summer garden red roses
ripe pears the old rock wall
three bluebirds landing the
grasses bowing to bees.

In that hot noon quiet our
land has a green scent it
was there I heard them
my holy Voices like music
I knelt...and it began....

EPILOGUE

JOAN'S WORDS

It is true that God sent me.

Oh, I appeal to God, the great judge,
from this great wrong and oppression.

Bishop, I die through you!

Master Peter, where shall I be this night?
By God's grace I shall be in Paradise.

What I said, I said for fear of the fire.

I was damning myself to save my life.

If I should say that God had not sent me
I should damn myself.

WHAT REMAINS

Look at her hang there
blackened and burned
still chained to that stake
a piece of charred meat

The fire is quenched now
to prove Joan is dead not
stolen away nor escaped
they order us to behold her

That sagging scarecrow
once a girl with eyelashes
fingers ears a beating heart
who dares to look at her now?

The fire is kindled once again
they burn what is left until
Joan is ashes and someone
will throw them into the Seine

Who will do it, we wonder ---
and will he sleep well tonight
after a drink with his dinner?
Which of us will sleep again?

Throughout our lives we will
see her as she hung there in
the sun like a black banner
and we will hear her scream

She is burned into our minds
now and there she will stay
our memory of this day will
be this girl's invisible grave

Other than us she has none
not a marker not a memorial
except in our dreams where
we must meet Joan again

AFTERMATH

BISHOP CAUCHON
ROUEN, 30 MAY 1431

Let me admit what I always feared most:
As we burn the Maid, we make a saint
and worse still a martyr, not merely toast.
Joan will be glorified; I will bear the taint

as "villain"—if I am even remembered
once this dramatic scene has played out
and my famous name is asunder.

I will stand before God with sins I flout

How I will be humbled and Hell-bound
while that peasant girl, that warrior maid
holds the Seraphim utterly spellbound
because of me, the betrayer betrayed.

If peasants be sainted by burning
I surrender my own saintly yearning.

STUDENT WRITING A PAPER ON JOAN

Hello? I'm stuck. The assignment,
what else? I started
with her execution but it's so gross,
burning someone alive. A sicko,
that bishop, or ambitious or both.
Then I went back to her heresy trial.
Okay, she was cool but it was
rigged, it was boring. I sort of got
into it with her Voices. Like
maybe that part was real and
we just don't get it. No, I *don't*
think she was nuts. One
guy, a military type, wrote that
she was a great leader, had a
tactical mind. Yeah, she was
our age. But here's the
thing, I'd sign any paper to
get myself off. And I wouldn't
take it back like she did.
Okay, I know a hero dies
instead of living a lie. But to
burn at the stake? Not me.
So what did you write?

SCULPTOR Of "THE MAID"

I refuse to carve you astride a horse.
Too many statues of you look like that.
I view you as a bird, no helmet, no hat,
waiting to die, tremulous, never coarse.

Joan, I chisel away at your breasts,
and see you as a girl without armor,
stunned that a Bishop would harm her
in God's name but weary of protest.

I am falling in love with you, fair Maid;
we all fall for you, then and now.
we want a shard of your shine but how
can we touch one holy renegade?

I touch you somehow in this stone
and hope scraps of light may transfer
and this I ask but you do not answer
so I finish those breasts you disown.

What is the mystery of you, my Joan?
You were hypnotic in your own age
and still we reach toward your image,
you who are ageless, we hope to clone.

Could your Voices address *us* now
or is it a new voice we hear: yours?
You might speak of God or of wars
but to listen we have to know how.

Joan, I carve your knees bending
in prayer as mine do not and you
understand this because you knew
I knelt in your Light unending.

ROUEN, FRANCE 2014

Elusive Joan,
a statue stands near the
place where you burned
but we can't capture you
not now not yet not ever
except as Mystery

Determined Joan,
you defy what we know
when we try to categorize:
whacko dreamer maid we
don't get the juice of you
Why do we fail?

Evasive Joan,
we can't put you in a box
Exhibit A: Holy crackpot
Exhibit B: Heretic saint
Exhibit C: Soldier maid
All/none of the above?

Gutsy Joan,
this much we can say:
a farmer's daughter you
led armies to triumph and
died by fire for your faith
We say: It is what it is.

Enigma, Joan,
we want to know you
but on our own terms
though we analyze you
and we dramatize you
we miss the point.

Mystical Joan,
I can't hear your Voices
but they guided you
and you guided men
and you guide us still
when we try to be brave

TONIGHT

You there
kneeling by your bed
white night gown pooling
around you like cream

While you
open yourself in prayer
seeking God's will for
your wandering life

You wait
to give the fruit of you
like a peeled peach
served on a platter

But you
must look at the risk
in your pure offer
all fruit is consumed

You know
or maybe you don't
I too burned with faith
and for faith I burned

Now you
take your turn to be
God's torch on earth
until you burn out

You see
when that happens
it is not the end
to burn is to live
you die giving light

NOON TODAY

Can you hear me?
don't be afraid
this isn't a dream
have no doubts

Once I stood like you
in my father's garden
at noon and there I
too heard a Voice.

I was sent to you
with a call from God
don't speak of it yet
few—understand.

I was afraid at first
but that passes fast
I will visit you often
to help you believe.

God sees your soul
you asked for a Sign
I come to guide you
as once I was guided.

I am a messenger
God will be with you
if you say *Yes* or *No*
Can you hear me now?

Your mission is this....

BIBLIOGRAPHY

Belloc, Hillaire: *Joan of Arc*

Brooks, Polly Schoyer: *Beyond the Myth: The Story of Joan of Arc*

Fraioli, Debora: *Joan of Arc and the Hundred Years War*

Nash-Marshall, Siobhan: *Joan of Arc: A Spiritual Biography*

Péguy, Charles: *The Mystery of the Charity of Joan of Arc*

Pernoud, Regine: *Joan of Arc: By Herself and Her Witnesses*

Shaw, George B.: *Saint Joan*

Trask, Willard (Translator): Joan of Arc in Her Own Words

Twain, Mark: *Joan of Arc, Personal Reflections of Joan of Arc*

Warner, Marina: *Joan of Arc: The Image of Female Heroism*

<u>**Critical Acclaim For Novels By Marcy Heidish**</u>

A WOMAN CALLED MOSES

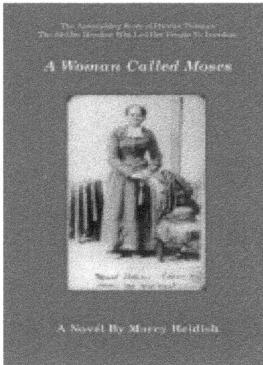

*Award-winning, best-selling novel based on the life of Harriet Tubman, abolitionist and conductor on the Underground Railroad.

*Literary Guild Alternate Selection;

*A Bantam paperback.

*TV Movie, starring Cicely Tyson, still available on DVD.

*Houghton Mifflin Co., 1st Pub.

<u>Praise for *A Woman Called Moses*:</u>

Publishers Weekly: "Her story has been told before, but never as eloquently, almost poetically, as here...achingly real...a strong narrative of a totally committed woman, one who speaks directly to our own desperate need to feel committed—and our wish that somewhere in the world there were more people like Harriet Tubman."

Washington Post Book World: "Profoundly rewarding...a daring work of the imagination."

Chicago Sun Times: "Marcy Heidish has, almost uncannily, crawled into the skin and very mind of Harriet Tubman. The dialogue sings with poetic beauty."

Houghton Mifflin Co.: "As events build toward a stunning climax, we are drawn into the spellbinding narrative of an extraordinary life, and a portion of our American past." ◆◆◆

WITNESSES

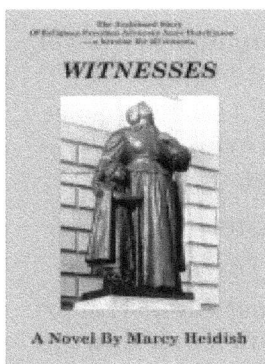

* Award-winning novel based on the life of lay minister Anne Hutchinson, <u>America's first female advocate of religious freedom</u>.

* Citations: Society for Colonial Wars; laudatory reviews; large-print, hard-cover and paperback versions.

* Houghton Mifflin Co., 1stPub.

<u>Praise for *Witnesses*:</u>

The New York Times Book Review: " .nothing ordinary about her creation of this remarkable woman. The novel abounds in literary grace. It employs the voices of the times as though heard this minute."

The New Yorker Magazine: "A striking novel...a compelling portrait."

The Washington Post: "Pure pleasure. Anne Hutchinson is real; thanks to *Witnesses,* she at last assumes her proper place in American history."
—Jonathan Yardley, Pulitzer Prize-winning critic.

Ballantine Books: "This fearless woman, mother of fifteen, a leader in medicine and politics, comes to vivid life in these pages. A true believe in religious freedom who paid dearly for her principles in two trials for heresy. In the tradition of Arthur Miller's *The Crucible*, Witnesses is the deeply felt portrait of a woman in the paranoid climate of 17th century Boston." ◆◆◆

THE TORCHING—The Book Store Murders

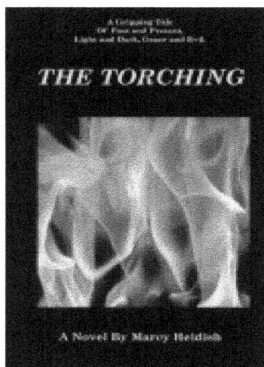

THE TORCHING

A Novel By Marcy Heidish

* Acclaimed contemporary novel, in hardcover and paperback.

* Literary Guild Alternate Selection; laudatory reviews.

* Optioned for TV movie.

* Simon & Schuster, 1st Pub.

Praise for *The Torching*:

Washington Post Book World: "Because of Heidish's skill, we get the full force of her double-whammy.in part due to the grace with which she weaves the present-day and the historical, but also because of her inventiveness at the book's close, the daring way she gets both strands of plot to unite...a stylish and intelligent novelist to boot, more than up to the dizzying, tale-spinning task that she set for herself here."

Kirkus Reviews: "Shuddery mystery-suspense with supernatural overtones."

Library Journal:"Intricately constructed. A deliciously spine-tingling, multi-layered literary mystery."

Publishers Weekly: "Subtle, gratifying psychologi-cal suspense. Penetrating characterizations... Heidish impeccably orchestrates the historical and contemporary, the supernatural and psychological."

Denver Post: "Macabre ride...Eerie.Intriguing. Frightening surprises...Enjoy."

Arizona Daily Star: "An imaginative, amazing writer...A magician with words."

New York Daily News: "Compellingly readable and likely to induce the screaming-meemies." ♦♦♦

THE SECRET ANNIE OAKLEY

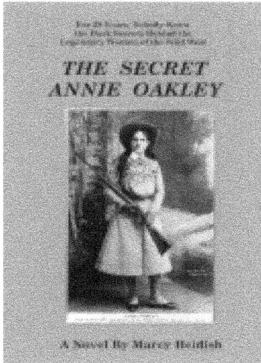

* Acclaimed novel based on the life of the legendary sharp-shooter.

* Hard- and Paperback versions

* A *Readers Digest* Condensed Novel.

* Optioned for film.

*Translated into several languages, laudatory reviews.

*New American Library, 1st Pub.

Praise for *The Secret Annie Oakley:*

Kirkus Reviews: "An immensely touching and cohesive fictional biography of the legendary sharp-shooter.builds from exemplary research to a fresh portrait of a talented woman in crisis.a class act—as Heidish reconstructs. with color and drama, the choreography of the shows, the tone of the period, and the textures of a haunting past."

The Arizona Daily Star: "...an imaginative, amazing writer.a magician with words. Each character has been brought to life with a mere pen stroke; flesh and blood beings that are more than fiction. A masterpiece of creative writing."

The Kansas City Star: "An unforgettable story."

Christian Science Monitor: "...Marcy Heidish weaves historical facts into a novel so moving that there will be many times in the years to come that I'll take pleasure in remembering that stout-hearted woman. 'Annie Oakley' hits the bull's eye every time."
◆◆◆

MIRACLES

MIRACLES

A Novel By Marcy Heidish

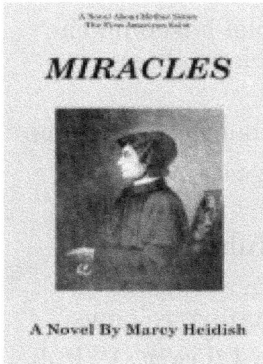

* Historical novel based on the life of **Mother Elizabeth Seton**, first American-born canonized saint.

* Main selection, *The Catholic Book Club.*

*New American Library, 1ˢᵗ Pub.

Praise for *Miracles*:

The New York Times Book Review: "This appealing book, told from the point of view of a skeptical modern priest, moves swiftly through tragedy to triumph."

Kirkus Reviews: "Working delicately with a balance of Church hagiography and psychological insight, Ms. Heidish provides another strong focus on the root dilemma of female saints and achievers."

New American Library: "*Miracles* is the story of an unforgettable woman's life and love. It is a novel charged with the vitality of a life that saw many changes, and with the power of a love that took many forms.[whether] as a lonely daughter of a wealthy, indifferent man; a searching young woman; a contented matron embracing a marriage that produced five beloved children; a widow searching for new meaning to life." ♦♦♦

DEADLINE

DEADLINE

A Novel Of Suspense
By Marcy Heidish

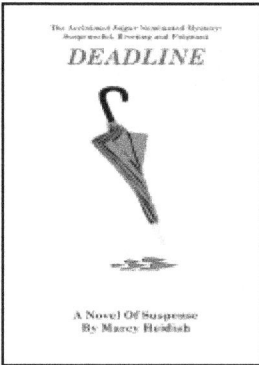

* Contemporary psychological novel with a "mystery" as a narrative line.

* Nominee for prestigious national "Edgar" Award; fine reviews.

* St. Martin's Press, 1ˢᵗ Pub.

Praise for *Deadline*:

Washington Post: "*Deadline* is a tense, well-turned tale, filled with authentic police and newspaper people. Heidish's taut, punchy style moves the story at lightning speed."

Kirkus Reviews: "The high-tension plot is enhanced by sharply etched pictures, by many vivid characters, and by a crisp, clean, first-person style. Heidish imbues her haunting story and her gutsy heroine with a rare sense of tenderness and poignancy. An impressive mystery by a gifted writer."

St. Martin's Press: "This wire-tight novel probes relentlessly, driving deep into psychological darkness and violent death. As the riveting story reaches its stunning conclusion, we see a complex woman forced to meet the ultimate deadline." ◆◆◆

A Dangerous Woman: Mother Jones, An Unsung American Heroine

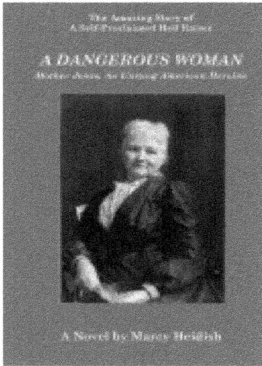

*A compelling, inspiring new historical novel, another powerful "profile in courage" American-style novel based on the life of Mary Harris Jones, a self-proclaimed Hell Raiser, daring labor leader, and colorful, quirky humanitarian.

*The arresting novel of an indomitable force, dressed demurely in widow's weeds and lace collars who:

> As an Irish immigrant—lost her homeland to the Great Famine.

> As a wife and mother—lost her whole family to yellow fever.

> As a dressmaker—lost home and business to the Chicago Fire

> As a survivor—turned from sorrow to help others survive.

Follow one of America's most feisty, fearless.and forgotten heroines whose rallying cry was:

"PRAY FOR THE DEAD—AND FIGHT LIKE HELL FOR THE LIVING!" ♦♦♦

DESTINED TO DANCE: A Novel About Martha Graham

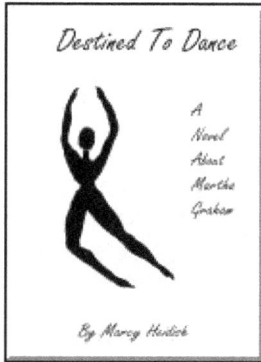

> They called her a genius.

> They called her a goddess.

> They called her a monster.

Which title best fits Martha Graham, iconic Mother of Modern Dance? Find out—in the <u>first historical novel about this great American diva</u>.

DESTINED TO DANCE is a creative portrait of the legendary dancer and choreographer. Heidish offers another remarkable account of an American hero– ine: her successes, her sorrows, and her struggles.

Here is a masterful portrait of Graham, on stage, backstage, offstage. We see Graham's break-through brilliance, often compared to Picasso's or Stravinsky.

We also witness Graham's triumph over alcoholism, despair, and a failed marriage. Set against the intriguing world of dance, Martha Graham's story offers us a close-up on a complex and compelling overcomer.

Martha Graham (1894-1991) invented a new "language of movement," still taught around the world and exemplified in such classic works as *Appalachian Spring*, among 180 others.

As always, Heidish's research is thorough and her sense of her subject is magical. For all who love the arts, all who seek inspiration, and all who like to read between history's lines, ***DESTINED TO DANCE*** is a must-read book.   ◆◆◆

NON-FICTION BOOKS:
Soul and the City
WaterBrook Press, Random House imprint

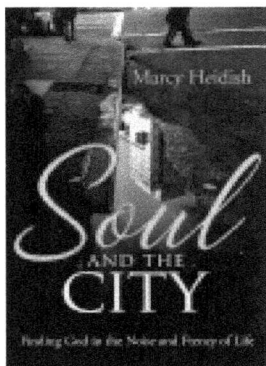

Praise for *Soul and the City*:

*"I actually started reading Marcy Heidish's *Soul and the City* on a subway train. I must say it had exactly the effect she writes about: it gave me peace in the middle of the hurry, the rush, the loud noise of the city."

—Rick Hamlin, executive editor, Guideposts; author of *Finding God on the A Train*

* "Marcy Heidish has compiled a rich and nuanced touring companion to rival any Michelin or Eye-witness guide—usable in any city of the world. Keep it close and.you will meet beauty and holiness no matter where you pause to look."

— Leigh McLeroy, author of *The Beautiful Ache* and *The Sacred Ordinary*

* "*Soul and the City* is a deeply inspiring call to awareness to connection with God and with others, and ultimately to soulful worship through so many aspects of life in the city that we find mundane, undesirable, or that even go unnoticed. Almost instantly, upon delving into its pages, you find your perspective changed."

— Sarah Zacharias Davis, author of *Confes-sions from an Honest Wife, Transparent,* and *The Friends We Keep.*   ♦♦♦

Defiant Daughters
Liguori Publications.

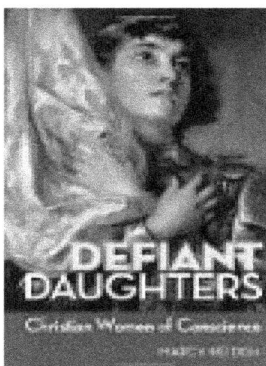

<u>Praise for *Defiant Daughters*</u>:

What do
Joan of Arc,
Immaculée Ilibagiza,
Corrie ten Boom, and
Sojourner Truth
have in common?

These women are among those whom best-selling author Marcy Heidish calls "Defiant Daughters."

This informative, challenging, and entertaining book spotlights the lives of more than 20 spiritual trail-blazers and their responses to crises of conscience.

They represent different races, denominations, and nations, but all are feisty—often fiery—and always faithful to their callings.

Heidish seeks out the decisive juncture where each took a stand for conscience, however high the cost.

This stunning and compelling book will bring you face-to-face with an unforgettable female gallery of "profiles in courage."

— Liguori Publications ♦♦♦

A Candle At Midnight
Ave Maria Press

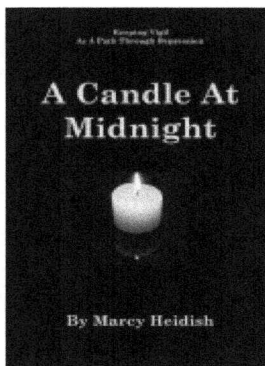

Prase for *A Candle At Midnight*:

* "Heidish honors modern medicine and spiritual healing in this compelling work."

— Alen J. Salerian, M.D., Medical Director of the Washington Psychiatric Center

* "This is not a book of abstractions. I recommend this book to anyone who is caught in the darkness of mid-night."

— Martha Manning, Author of *Undercurrents: A Life Beneath the Surface*:

* "A masterpiece!"

— Rev. Nancy Eggert, Spiritual Director   ♦♦♦

Who Cares? Simple Ways YOU Can Reach Out

Ave Maria Press

Praise for *Who Cares?*:

A lonely neighbor, a colleague in distress, a friend in difficulty. In situations like these we want to reach out and help, yet so often we feel unsure about our response.

What to do?

What to say?

What is enough?

Too much?

Too little?

This practical book is designed to bring out the caring person in each of us. Marcy Heidish offers simple, specific ways to practice the art of caring, especially within our immediate circle of concern: family, friends, neighbors, and coworkers.

Heidish reminds us of the many little things we can do to open the door to a caring relationship.

— **Ave Maria Press**

"Contains savvy insights and wisdom about service. This is an ideal resource for anyone interested in engaged spirituality."

— *Cultural Information Service*: ♦♦♦

Too Late To Be A Fortune Cookie Writer

"A novelist has a specific poetic license which also applies to his own life."

~ Jerzi Kosinski

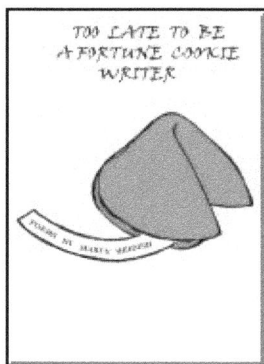

Marcy Heidish, award-winning author of fourteen books, fiction and non-fiction, is just such a novelist with a "specific poetic license."

Her work has been praised for its "lyrical grace" and so it is a special joy to present her first book of poetry. Ms. Heidish has written poems for decades.

With humor and humanity, this collection spans a broad range of subjects. Insight, wit and depth enliven these poems. They address universal concerns: maturity, mortality, memory and much more.

Ms. Heidish gives us an intimate glimpse into a writer's soul. Adept at varied verse forms, she amuses, reflects, recalls, and rejoices:

• "A watched pot never boils unless you're boiling vodka."

• "Houses crowd my life like chairs on a November beach."

• "The sun is a peach, half ripened, at hand."

And the poet brings us with her. ♦♦♦

Scene Through A Window
A Historical Romance

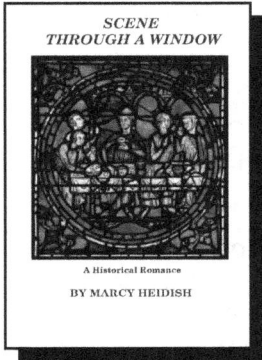

Travel through the centuries to watch a timeless love unfold around a timeless masterpiece: the fabled cathedral of Chartres, France. In 1194, an unthinkable disaster struck that sacred site. In one June night, a firestorm devastated the cathedral, its artwork, and parts of its surrounding town.

Immediately, the finest artists converged on Chartres to plan a new and innovative structure, built to endure and to surpass all that went before. Inevitably, these plans led to plots and rivalry, threatening the realization of a daring and demanding dream.

Against this backdrop, two lovers struggle to conceive the new cathedral's stained glass windows, still regarded as marvels today. This quest centers on discovering new gem-like colors: unique, precious, and incomparable. The pair, under increasing pressure, embarks on an intense search for the mysterious but elusive answers

Deftly weaving fact with fiction, Marcy Heidish sets an inspirational love story against a thoroughly researched Medieval backdrop. With her proven attention to detail, Heidish transports us to the winding streets of Chartres: its sounds and smells, its interiors and intrigues. Suspenseful, engrossing, and imaginative, *Scene Through A Window* creates a magical space where the impossible can happen.

Short Pieces:

Articles and book reviews published in *Ms.* Magazine, *GEO* Magazine, *The Washington Post*, *The Washington Star*, and various in-flight periodicals. Two of these pieces are:

* *The Pilgrim Who Stayed*, *GEO* Magazine, about Chartres Cathedral, widely translated.

* *The Grand Dame of the Harbor*, about the Statue of Liberty, was a highly acclaimed cover story for *GEO* Magazine. This article is included in a textbook anthology designed to teach writing to college students. Winner of coveted Apex Award. ♦♦♦

See Marcy Heidish page at:
www.Amazon.com
[AND Kindle] *

* Marcy Heidish Books are printed by Lightning Source and distributed by Ingram of Ingram Content Group Inc., the world's largest distributor of physical and digital content, providing books, music and media content to over 38,000 retailers, libraries, schools and distribution partners in 195 countries. More than 25,000 publishers use Ingram's . ♦♦♦

www.ingramcontent.com/pod-product-compliance
Lightning Source LLC
Chambersburg PA
CBHW071451070426
42452CB00039B/1031